D1402133

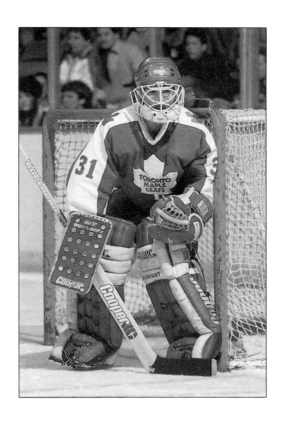

TORONTO
MAPLE LEAFS

CHRYS GOYENS

Published by Creative Education
123 South Broad Street, Mankato, Minnesota 56001
Creative Education is an imprint of The Creative Company.

Designed by Rita Marshall
Cover Illustration by Rob Day

Photos by: Bettmann Archives, Bruce Bennett Studios, Hockey Hall of
Fame and Wide World Photos

Library of Congress Cataloging-in-Publication Data

Goyens, Chrys.
Toronto Maple Leafs / Chrys Goyens.
p. cm. — (NHL today)
ISBN 0-88682-689-6

1. Toronto Maple Leafs (Hockey team)—History—Juvenile literature.
[1. Toronto Maple Leafs (Hockey team)—History. 2. Hockey—History.]
I. Title. II. Series.

GV848.T6G69   1995   94-1361
796.962'64'09713541—dc20

123456

A GLORIOUS RIDE

In the 1992–93 National Hockey League season, the Toronto Maple Leafs achieved a startling transformation. In a single season, they went from being a team with a history to one with a future. Prior to the 1993 playoffs, the last season to offer any hope was 1977–78, when the Leafs tied their all-time points mark with 92 and upset the New York Islanders in the NHL quarter-finals, only to be swept in four games by the eventual champion Canadiens in the semifinals.

Doug Gilmour played in two consecutive All-Star Games.

1 9 2 6

Conn Smythe purchased the Maple Leafs and served as their first coach.

From that season through 1991–92, Toronto's record was dismal: in 14 seasons, the club played .346 hockey, missed the playoffs six times, lost the first playoff series five times and advanced to a second series, which they lost, three times.

And then came the Great Turnaround of 1992–93. All year, the Leafs stayed near the top of the league standings. Torontonians scarcely dared to breathe loudly in March and April, afraid to burst a fragile bubble of success. They need not have worried. The Leafs went down to the wire with Chicago and Detroit and finished third in the division, which meant they would play the second-place Red Wings in the first round of the playoffs.

Seven games of up-and-down, ferocious entertainment resulted. However, with less than three minutes left in Game 7 at Detroit's Joe Louis Arena, Detroit led 3-2. Things looked bleak for the Leafs, but Doug Gilmour simply wouldn't let the Leafs fall.

"He's our soul," coach Pat Burns said. "We'll only go as far as Doug will take us." The question of the moment was simple: where could Gilmour take Toronto in three short minutes?

"The more I played, the more I wanted to play," said Gilmour. But as he lined up for a face-off late in the game, his proud shoulders were slumped, his cheeks were hollow with fatigue and it seemed he couldn't skate another step.

Great players have a way of overcoming obstacles. At 17:17 Gilmour took a pass in the high slot and snapped a quick shot into the Detroit net. Then, at 2:35 of overtime, Gilmour outmuscled a much larger Detroit defender and sent a pass back to the blue line. Defenseman Bob Rouse slapped the puck at the net without hesitating and a diminutive Russian winger named Nikolai Borschevsky deflected it home.

Dave Andreychuk is one of the Maple Leafs' top scorers (page 7).

Ace Bailey led the league in scoring points at the end of the regular season.

Two weeks later, the Leafs repeated the exploit against St. Louis, and the whole town was agog at the prospect of Toronto's first semifinal in 15 years. It was a third straight emotional rollercoaster for Toronto fans, and they were in agony when the Leafs surrendered a 3-2 series lead to the Kings in Los Angeles on Wayne Gretzky's overtime winner in Game 6, forcing yet another seventh game.

"Doug Gilmour played the entire playoffs like he was from another planet; he was exceptional," said Gretzky, "and I was playing with a bit of desperation myself. If we would have lost in Game 6, no matter what I would have done for the rest of my career, the people back in my home province would have brought that up—'Yeah, but you lost that series to Toronto; where was Wayne Gretzky against the Leafs?'—I didn't want to hear that talk for years."

Late in the third period of Game 7, with the score tied at 3-3 and sudden-death overtime beckoning, Gretzky struck quickly with his second and third goals of the game to give Los Angeles what appeared to be an insurmountable 5-3 lead.

Could the Leafs come back one last time? With 74 seconds left in the game, Toronto scored and hope soared at Maple Leaf Gardens. But in the game's final 20 seconds, with their goalie replaced by an extra attacker, the Leafs' final attack in the Kings' end died on the outside of a goalpost. This time there would be no miracle. The great, glorious ride was over.

As in other seasons, the Leafs had been eliminated. However, there was one major difference this time—the Leafs were back, and the hockey world knew it. This team would be around for a long time.

During the 1600s and 1700s, Native Americans used the land connecting Lake Ontario and Lake Huron as an overland route, vital to their existence. Later, this site was chosen to be the capital of the Canadian province we now know as Ontario. In 1834 this settlement was named Toronto, a Huron Indian word for "meeting place."

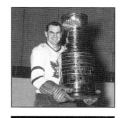

Syl Apps won the Calder Memorial Trophy as the NHL's most outstanding rookie.

Toronto has more than lived up to its name. Today the city is the chief communications, manufacturing and financial center of Canada. It has the largest metropolitan population in the nation, is one of Canada's busiest ports and is also a major cultural center. The city's towering skyline gives notice that this is a city for the next century.

Toronto is a meeting place for sports, too. The Toronto Blue Jays of baseball's American League are two-time defending champions of the World Series. The Toronto Argonauts of the Canadian Football League play in the city and a National Basketball Association franchise was awarded to Toronto in late 1993. But of all the professional sports teams in Toronto, it is the Maple Leafs that have the longest history.

The early story of the Leafs is largely the story of Conn Smythe, whose name is on the trophy honoring the top performer in the playoffs each year. In 1926 he bought the Toronto St. Patricks, a team that was first organized in 1917 as an original member of the National Hockey League. He promptly changed the club's name to the Maple Leafs.

While North America suffered through the early years of the Great Depression, Smythe and Frank Selke ordered the construction of a new arena for the team. When the building was opened on

Dave Andreychuk is one of the stars of the 90s (pages 10-11).

Turk Broda won his first of two Vezina Trophies as the league's top goaltender.

November 12, 1931, the Leafs were ready to fly. "The Kid Line" of Joe Primeau, Charlie Conacher and Harvey "Busher" Jackson was the catalyst of a powerhouse team that also included Hall-of-Famers Frank "King" Clancy and Ace Bailey, Red Horner, Clarence "Hap" Day and Lorne Chabot. The Leafs christened the new building in style, winning the Stanley Cup there in 1932.

Although the team remained competitive over the next decade, ten years passed before Toronto's second Cup parade. Coached by Hap Day, the Leafs defeated the Detroit Red Wings in a seven-game Stanley Cup final, regarded as one of the most thrilling in hockey history. The Leafs did in that 1942 series what no other team had ever done before. They came back to win four straight games after being down three games to none.

The Leafs again won the Cup in 1945. But then they started to flounder, and Smythe decided it was time to rebuild. Led by stars like Syl Apps, Ted "Teeder" Kennedy, Walter "Turk" Broda, Gus Mortson, Bill Ezinicki, Max Bentley and Bill Barilko, the juggernaut team reeled off four championships in five years between 1946 and 1951. "This is the greatest team I've ever had," said Smythe.

1 9 5 9

Punch Imlach coached the team from 1959 to 1969, compiling 365 wins, 270 losses and 125 ties.

PUNCH, THE BIG M AND A SPARKPLUG NAMED KEON

During the next decade, the best Toronto could do was two appearances in the finals, which resulted in two quick exits at the hands of the archrival Montreal Canadiens. Smythe was anxious to have his team return to the glory days of old when he reached into the Boston Bruins organization for the team's newest savior—veteran coach and hockey man George "Punch" Imlach.

Imlach was hired in 1958 as general manager and was named coach the next year. He was a scrappy Torontonian with a big nose and a bald spot he covered with his trademark fedora. He had paid his dues in two decades of coaching, which included a stop with the Quebec Aces of the Quebec Senior League, where his star had been the legendary captain of the Montreal Canadiens, Jean Beliveau.

Imlach's first move as general manager was to build a veteran defense: Johnny Bower in goal and Allan Stanley, Bob Baun, Tim Horton, Marcel Pronovost and Carl Brewer on the blue line. Up front, the Leafs were an exciting mix of young talent and veteran savvy, with Frank Mahovlich, Dave Keon, Bob Pulford, Eddie Shack, Ron Stewart, Tod Sloan, Dick Duff and Red Kelly.

Pete Stemkowski joined the team at center, adding 93 points in 221 games.

Mahovlich and Keon were the jewels of the collection. Mahovlich, a tall, fluid skater who never seemed to rush but who ate up miles of ice with huge, graceful strides, was known throughout the hockey world as "the Big M." He won the Calder Trophy in the 1957–58 season as the league's top rookie, and in 1961 scored 48 goals during an exciting season-long scoring battle with Montreal's Bernard Geoffrion, who managed 50.

Mahovlich was so good that the Chicago Blackhawks offered Toronto $1 million for his services, at a time when $7,500 a year was a good salary in the sport. The Leafs, wisely, turned down the offer.

Keon had a very different style. The tiny center was the quintessential waterbug, darting here and there and harassing the opposition all over the rink. He paid the price for disturbing slower—and much bigger—adversaries, yet still came at them, scars and all.

"Frank Mahovlich might have been the engine of the Leafs in the early 1960s," Smythe was fond of saying. "But Davey Keon's our sparkplug. Without him, the engine wouldn't run."

And run it did. After the Blackhawks ended the Montreal Canadiens' bid for a sixth straight Stanley Cup in 1961, it was Toronto's turn to shine. Imlach's rigid defensive system, gifted goal scorers and top goaltending came together for three straight years and Toronto went home with Cups in 1962, 1963 and 1964.

The next year, the Canadiens were back, reeling off a quick pair of Cups in 1965 and 1966. Then Toronto took over once more, defeating Montreal for the Cup in 1967. In that matchup Montreal was heavily favored, but Toronto's "Over the Hill Gang" (the squad had an average age of over 30 years) prevailed in six games,

Dave Keon won the Lady Byng Trophy in 1962 and 1963 (page 15).

thanks mainly to the heroics of veteran goalies Johnny Bower and Terry Sawchuk.

But that was Toronto's last gasp. By 1970, most of the veteran Leafs had been scattered to all corners of the new 14-team NHL, and Punch Imlach was en route to Buffalo.

THE GREATEST NIGHT EVER

The Leafs of the 1970s were competitive and exciting, but more on an individual level than as a team. As a result, they always came up short in the postseason chase for the Stanley Cup.

The players rarely could be faulted, however. During the 1970s and 1980s, the Leafs were the property of Harold Ballard, an ebullient and egocentric owner whose offbeat administrative decisions guaranteed a long line of lean years. Ballard's inconsistencies

Rick Ley tallied 62 points and 416 PIM over three seasons.   17

cost the franchise dearly, but still the faithful Leafs fans turned out in droves to cheer on their team.

And they had six good reasons to remain faithful: goalie Mike Palmateer, defensemen Ian Turnbull and Borje Salming, wingers Lanny McDonald and Dave "Tiger" Williams, and center Darryl Sittler. Together they were known as "the Magnificent Six." Sittler and McDonald have both since been inducted into the NHL Hall of Fame for their hockey heroics, and Salming's turn is coming.

One memorable game in 1976 best showed the power of the Magnificent Six—and the excitement they brought to Maple Leaf Gardens.

It was February 7, 1976, and the division-leading Boston Bruins were visiting. Rookie goalie Dave Reece faced the Leafs that night, and at the first intermission Boston was behind 2-0.

20

All Canada was abuzz after the second period. Sittler, who had assisted on the first-period goals, had exploded with three goals of his own and another pair of assists in the middle period, and was within one point of a single-game scoring record of eight points held by two Canadiens, Maurice "Rocket" Richard and Bert Olmstead. Thousands of fans wondered if they would witness history on this night.

"They weren't the only ones," Sittler recalled. "It was one of those nights where everything I touched either went in, or over to somebody else who scored. And there I was with a whole period remaining to tie or break the record."

He didn't need the 20 minutes. Forty-four seconds into the third period, Sittler circled wide around a defenseman, cut sharply toward the net and lifted a backhander past a startled Reece. Four goals, four assists and the record was tied. Two more goals followed and Sittler had the NHL's first scoring performance in double figures, 10 points on six goals and four assists. After that performance, Toronto's 11-4 win was actually anticlimactic!

Sittler went on to score five goals in a playoff game against Philadelphia that April, and he scored the winning goal in overtime for Canada in the first Canada Cup competition. But he never tasted champagne from the Stanley Cup, and the promise of a great team was never realized.

Jim Jones joined the team at center, helping the team to their first 40-win season since 1951.

THE SILVER FOX

One truth in professional sports transcends all others: There will be no All-Stars on the court, field or ice if there are no All-Stars in the front office.

Borje Salming scored a record 620 assists with Toronto.

If the Toronto Maple Leafs had floundered for a quarter of a century on the ice, it was because there was no leadership "upstairs" where the players are selected and the deals are made. After two decades of Harold Ballard's shenanigans, faithful Leafs fans wondered if they would ever see a firm hand at the helm, someone who could establish a plan for success and then implement it.

That top manager arrived on Canada Day, July 1, 1991, in the person of silver-haired Cliff Fletcher, a Montreal native with 25 years' experience with four NHL teams. Fletcher, known as "the Silver Fox," demanded and received the power he needed to act independently and was named president, chief operating officer and general manager of the hockey team.

Darryl Sittler finished an eleven year career with Toronto, scoring 916 points in 844 games.

In the first of two blockbuster trades, Fletcher acquired wingers Glenn Anderson and Craig Berube and All-Star goalie Grant Fuhr from the Edmonton Oilers. Berube didn't stay long; a few weeks later he was moved to Calgary along with five other Leafs for Doug Gilmour and fellow forward Kent Manderville, defensemen Jamie Macoun and Ric Nattress and goalie Rick Wamsley.

Fletcher traded away 10 players with a sum total of zero Stanley Cup rings among them while acquiring nine others who owned 14 championship rings.

The Leafs failed to make the playoffs that first Fletcher season, falling short by three points. But the Silver Fox's first Toronto team was the most competitive in a long time at Maple Leaf Gardens, and it was ready to move up in the NHL.

Left to right: Ed Olczyk, Rick Vaive, Mark Osborne, Al Iafrate.

Prior to his second Toronto season, Fletcher determined that incumbent coach Tom Watt was linked too closely with the team's losing era and that the team needed a veteran coach and a winner. That man turned out to be Pat Burns, then the coach of the Montreal Canadiens and a former policeman.

While a policeman near the Canadian capital of Ottawa, Burns had turned to coaching as an outlet from the stress related to his job. A "not very good" Junior B player before picking up the badge, Burns took to coaching quickly, advancing through the ranks of bantam and midget hockey until he was selected to coach the Hull Olympiques of the Quebec Major Junior Hockey League.

When Canadiens general manager Serge Savard was looking for a coach to handle the Canadiens farm team in Sherbrooke in 1987, he asked his scouts a simple question: "Who's the best coach in the province of Quebec?" That September, Burns took over his first professional team, and although officially he was on sabbatical from his police career, somehow he and Savard knew that his days of pounding the beat were over.

Two years and one American Hockey League championship later, Burns found himself behind the bench of the Canadiens. Would coaching the sport's most storied team and dealing with a voracious media horde represent too much pressure for him?

"Pressure is dealing with bank robbers, drug dealers and the like," Burns replied. "Dealing with hockey players and the media is not pressure."

Four years later, bank robbers and drug dealers were looking good to a coach desperate to escape the Canadiens' media

1 9 9 2

Pat Burns took over the coaching duties and led the team to their first winning season since 1979.

Doug Gilmour is one of the NHL's top scorers (pages 26-27).   25

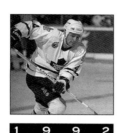

Dave Ellett scored an assist in his first All-Star Game appearance as a Maple Leaf.

fishbowl. When Fletcher came calling, Burns was Toronto-bound on the first available airplane.

Under Burns, the Leafs not only made the playoffs in 1992–93, they turned in the club's best performance with 44 wins, 29 losses and 11 ties for 99 points, seven more than any Toronto team had ever accomplished. While veteran stars like Doug Gilmour, Glenn Anderson, Wendel Clark and Peter Zezel led the way, a new coach and a rookie goaltender keyed the team's success.

Early in the season, goalie Grant Fuhr was injured and many Toronto fans felt that his absence would prevent the Leafs from making the playoffs. It may have been a blessing in disguise because rookie Felix Potvin—whose catlike reflexes earned him the name "Felix the Cat," after a popular cartoon character—stepped into the breach and played inspired hockey that kept the team near the top of its division until Fuhr returned. His thanks was a quick return to the American Hockey League, the NHL minors.

"He needed to play a lot, and with Grant back in Toronto that wouldn't happen," said Burns. "After all, Fuhr was a proven veteran with a big salary and we had to play him. I also told Felix that he was our goalie of the future and would be in Toronto for many years to come."

And then Fuhr was injured a second time.

Potvin returned to Toronto and played superbly. General managers around the league began making inquiries about the availability of Potvin and/or Fuhr in trade talks. "One indicator that Felix had arrived was that some of these people asked about Felix first, and not Fuhr," Fletcher said. When Fuhr returned, he was dealt to Buffalo and the Leafs acquired another huge piece for their puzzle: hulking Dave Andreychuk, slow of foot but a deadly scorer on the power play, and a veteran with more than 300 NHL goals to his credit.

It was an inspired transaction, allowing Potvin to play every day and Andreychuk to score 25 goals in 31 games with Toronto for a career-high total of 54 at season's end. But how could a new coach entrust his team's fortunes to a rookie netminder?

"Confidence," Potvin answered with characteristic candor.

"Pat and I don't talk a lot, but then we don't have to," he continued. "I have confidence in him, and he has confidence in me. There isn't much to say beyond that."

Potvin proved his mettle in the playoffs as Toronto defeated Detroit and St. Louis before succumbing to Los Angeles. All three series went seven games, the goaltender's version of a torture chamber.

"When it was over, Felix was the same guy he's always been," Burns said. "That gave me a lot of confidence looking ahead to the next season."

Wendel Clark scored on a penalty shot against Trevor Kidd of the Flames.

Mike Gartner is fifth in goal-scoring in the NHL.

Rookie Damian Rhodes posted a 9-7-3 record in 1993-94.   31

That confidence was warranted as Potvin had 34 wins in 1993–94, fifth in the entire league and tying a 34-year-old team record for wins in one season. Overall the Leafs finished second in their division with a strong 43-29-12 record. They were the only team to reach the Stanley Cup semifinals for two straight years, defeating Chicago and San Jose before succumbing to Vancouver.

In 1994, looking to rejuvenate his team even more, Fletcher traded his popular captain Wendel Clark to Quebec for a 6-foot-4 Swedish scoring machine named Mats Sundin. Other players expected to contribute to the team's success include Nikolai Borschevsky, Kent Manderville and Drake Berehowsky.

After a quarter-century long hiatus, the Leafs are back to legendary form, with Pat the Cop and Felix the Cat leading the way. Toronto fans are optimistic that the future holds a Stanley Cup—and plenty of exciting hockey.

1 9 9 5

Toronto is looking to other new players like Yanic Perreault, who played his rookie season in Toronto in 1994.